Our Life on the "A" List

By R. E. Forbes

ISBN: 978-0-578-17754-0

Published by Rachel E. Forbes

Foreword

Maybe it all starts with me. Maybe it all starts with the two year-old me who didn't see the need to talk to other people, who preferred to observe and analyze instead. Maybe it starts with the three, four, and five year-old me staring at the television wondering why the smug roadrunner kept tormenting the coyote, why the roadrunner and coyote and the cat and mouse were locked in a perpetual, meaningless chase- all while my brother, sister, and cousins rolled on the floor laughing in hysteria.

Maybe, it all starts with one of my parents, or maybe, it all starts with one of their parents.

No matter where it originates, Asperger's is. I have had to learn that. It doesn't go away. It can't be quieted or hushed without severe consequence. It isn't readily explained. I have had to accept that I cannot fix it. I cannot heal it or send it into remission. It's something that my son will live with for the rest of his life. And so my son and I are learning to live our best lives within autism's presence.

My journey with a son who has Asperger Syndrome is less about my son and the diagnosis and more about how I am learning to adjust to be the sort of parent he needs to lead him towards his path to functionality. As I write now, he is a junior class president, he is a hardworking honor-roll student, he is taking or has taken college-level course work in English, physics, calculus, and history, he enjoys and participates in robotics, he actively works on building meaningful friendships and being respectful, he actively works on controlling his emotions, he listens, he loves life, he volunteers, and he just simply enjoys being a regular old teenager.

Allow time to remove fifteen years from our existence, and this image of him blurs with each passing day. Quite frankly, a betting person would not have put money on my ability to rear a child with autism. I faced a lot of challenges growing up. I have never in my life been in a consistent place of financial stability. If I had my choice to do anything, I would spend all day thinking, writing, and researching. I could never be accused of being a social butterfly. I never planned to be the woman who had lots of kids. I wasn't even sure if I wanted any. I am most interested in serving my individual purpose for being here, my life's work. Anything outside of that, I consider to be a distraction. I wanted, I physically needed the singular mental space within which I could focus on manifesting my dreams. I couldn't do that when I was young. My family and I had a difficult time in those years.

In short, I don't seem like the ideal candidate for rearing a child whose disability revolves around social cognition and who requires mounds of patience and tenacity. But like many moms and dads who love their kids, I have always wanted the best for my son, so despite my challenges, I have learned to fight really hard to help him connect with the world so that he is able to find his niche, his place, his purpose.

There was a time when finding his purpose, however, wasn't even a consideration. Things were so bad that all I wanted was to be able to keep him alive and to have him accept the value in that endeavor. With respect to his right to tell his own story, I'll say that he functions well academically but has to work extremely hard to deal with the social and emotional challenges that present with the condition of Asperger's. It's hard for us. Not all of the time. Just when it is, it is.

Ebbs and flows- parents of children on the spectrum have to be ready for the endemic ebbs and flows. I was recently reminded that there will never be a time in my and my son's life when we don't have to filter life through the existence of autism. When I finally got my son back into school after homeschooling him for almost three years, I made the mistake of thinking that we were finished with the hard part. My advice to him had been focused on getting him to be able to function in school. But autism isn't like that. It doesn't fit neatly into simple back-to-school-night meet and greets. It doesn't tuck efficiently into the designated parent-teacher conference times that are manageable with only a few hours of leave from work a year. Autism is a lifelong battle. It roars at you through the phone to come to school immediately and at inopportune times in the work day. It impacts thoughts. It makes the autistic child think and rethink then rethink again about the same idea until he or she doesn't know what to do with that thought anymore. It impacts responses; it impacts perceptions; it impacts body movements; it impacts the ability to process information. Autism makes me pay it attention. It doesn't allow me to ignore it because I don't see the immediate impact it has on my son just by looking at him. Autism requires me to be present, to be alert, to be attentive, when I would rather be thinking, writing, and researching. It does not go quietly into the night, unless it does, and it's too late.

And so, I have always wanted to be ready for the ebbs and flows so that I can help my son and teach him and guide him towards greater and greater independence. I have always wanted him to see that he can live with autism. He can live a good life, his own good life. He can treasure himself. He can be confident enough to face a big scary world that seems filled with nothing but alien behavior.

I'm no expert. I'm just a mom who loves her kid, but that's probably more powerful than anything. My son and I are a work in progress, but we've come a long way. A lot of people ask me how my son and I have dealt with Asperger's, and so, I feel like just maybe, it's time for me to share what I've learned because our kids are special, and we know the struggle it takes to get them to performance, and we live with the reality that this is a lifelong journey. My hope is that through my sharing, some parent gathers the strength to keep on keeping on, for our wholeness as the parent is a key ingredient to our children's success.

It's not possible to explain our journey without telling our back story. As a result, I begin there because I think it's important for some parent out there who may have limited resources, who may not have support, who may be lost in this whole process to see that I have been there too and lived to tell about it. In the second part, I provide the strategies that I used to get my son to the level where he is now. I wanted to make sure that anybody who hears about our story understands the valid difficulty that living on the spectrum presents, but I also want to show that persistence, dedication, willingness to change and adapt, and hard work reap results.

I hope that our story can provide some usable information. There are no silver spoons here; there is lots of hard work, and there is dedication to achieving our goals; love undergirds everything. My point exactly: if we can do it, you can do it. You just have to find those strategies that work best for you and your child.

Part One

The race is not given

to the swift or the strong

but to those who endure to the end.

My Little Lumberjack

I was 25 and in a rough marriage, but I was getting ready to give birth. For many years and before I learned that I was pregnant, I had been a hard core feminist-womanist who despised and resisted any stereotypical "girly" behavior. But when I became pregnant, all I wanted to do was wear pink. It was the funniest revelation to me because I realized that I was in love like I had never experienced it before. I realized that no belief, no desire, no value system, nothing was more important than that little being growing inside of me.

When he finally got here, my son was nine pounds, two ounces, and twenty-one plus inches long. I called him my little lumberjack. My own mother took her first plane trip ever to come be with me and my son, to come watch over us for a little while as we started our journey together as mother and son.

I stayed at home with my son for the first year of his life. My husband at the time was in graduate school, and I was finishing my bachelor's degree. My whole goal had been to become a PhD, a writer, and a researcher. So, when I found out that I was pregnant, I decided that I would devote all of my energy to ensuring that the one child I had had a good life because I knew that I didn't want to have any more children- I was going to have that career I had dreamed of- just it would have to come as soon as my son was able to flourish.

Even though I stayed at home with my son and observed him every day, I still missed some very clear indicators that he was developing a bit differently. Everything seemed normal to me except for a few things. I just never recognized the differences as being characteristic of an overarching diagnosis.

First, when the nurse put my son on the table for Apgar testing, his father called to him. You have to know that we had spent a lot of time reading to him while he was in the womb, and we had told him who we were and who he was by name. As soon as his father called to him, my son looked like he was aware of his father's voice. It seems completely implausible, but it looked like my son isolated his father's voice and moved in response to it. We were shocked and discredited it as a reflex.

Once at home, I noticed that when I would hold him upright in my lap, he was so rigid that he stood on his legs. Then one day when he wasn't quite two months old, I tripped over the foot of my son's bassinet and made this sound like Homer Simpson makes when he makes a mistake, "D'oh!" My son burst out in a distinct but short laugh. It was a little scary because I didn't think that infants could respond that way. Yes, on a daily basis, I did talk to him about everything that I was doing with him. I talked to him about what we were buying in the grocery store, I talked to him about what he would feel as the water hit him when he took a bath, I warned him about how he'd feel when he had to take his shots, I told him about the letters and shapes and toys in his bedroom; I just talked about everything to make sure he knew what was going on. But I didn't think that that sort of stimulation would cause him to be verbal or laugh as an infant. When he was four months old, I had told him that his dad was getting ready to come home. As soon as his dad came through the door, he turned his head and said, "Hiiiiiii." Again, I tried to discredit what I'd heard, thinking that maybe what he said just sounded like "hi".

One day, when he was just about one and a half, I played the movie *Elmo in Grouchland.* When we got to the scene where Elmo lost his blanket, my son just lost it. He started screaming and throwing things. He was angry and hysterical. When I turned the movie off, he stopped. When I turned it back on to be sure that that had been the catalyst for his frustration, he became hysterical again. He did the same thing when I was looking at the movie *Dr. Doolittle* when the bear was in the bathroom with Eddie Murphy. He did the same thing if his father and I had an argument. All he had to do was perceive discord, and he would fly off the rails. It was crazy for me because it was all so unexpected. He was the happiest, fun-loving child, but when he sensed tension, he would lash out.

Can a Two Year-old Understand Divorce?

While I didn't know that my son had Asperger
Syndrome, I knew how badly he responded to anything
that he felt was disagreeable, and the arguments between
his father and me were becoming much too frequent and
the marriage was crumbling. I remember thinking that if
I left while my son was still very young, I could keep
him from being emotionally scathed. I always held the
memory of my own childhood. I didn't want my son to
live in confusion and chaos. I never wanted my son to
experience that sort of discord at my own hands.

When I was a teenager and my youngest brother was
born, I remember helping my mom with him. I would
read magazine articles, pore over them, and glean every
bit of information about child rearing and child
development from them that I could. You can imagine
that that didn't change when I had my son. I went to the
experts. I lived in the *What to Expect...* books and used
them to guide me through his first two years. My entire

focus was my son's wellbeing. That was just who I was and am. If I see a problem, it's about research, figuring out all of the components, and fixing all of the broken pieces; and if something is not broken, it's about understanding something so well that I understand how to maintain it. And that was my approach to motherhood- I wanted a happy kid, so I set about making that the reality.

As a result, my son's first two years were marked by happiness and celebrations. I remember waking up one morning and noticing that that little white bump had broken through his gum. That day became "Happy First Tooth Day". I had a photo shoot day once every month to document his first year. I established his sleep routine at one week old by using the houselights to simulate day so that I could keep him up until the permanent sleep time was established. Everything that the doctors told me, I did. I was obsessed with getting it right. I found self-worth in it. I breastfed. I bottle-fed to supplement. Fruits and vegetables, milk and juice, balanced proteins, healthy snacks- I never left home without them. Daily exercise, daily stimulation, daily fresh air, weekly trips to play areas for social interaction, parties with playmates, long rides across campus in his little bike trailer with his father or I glancing back to check on him, stopping to get ice cream, stopping to feed ducks, stopping to hear the river flow over rocks and kiss banks; every outing was framed as an adventure. It was a deliberate, fashioned life, all to make sure that he was happy.

By the time my son was about a year and a half, however, I knew that the marriage could not continue if I was going to be able to rear my son in a calm household. I remember that last Thanksgiving. I had cooked a really good meal, and we'd had a very nice day, one of those exceptional days that exists opposite the normal rancor, one of those days that makes you think that you just might be able to salvage what you thought was lost- and then all of a sudden, something changes. Out of nowhere an argument ensued, and my son immediately began to react. He started ripping papers from the desk and throwing them all over the floor. He was screaming in anger, and I can still see him bending over the papers, his little fingers strewing them angrily, his little voice yelling. I couldn't let him grow up that way, and I thought if I found a way to get out of the situation, then my son would have a chance.

I was reeling. My whole life, I was reeling- no peace at home, problems and unrest were always looming. I was reeling- always on the brink of losing it. Even my relationship with God was thwarted and had to be filtered because of my upbringing. Growing up, there was this strong emphasis on faith, but it came at the expense of doing anything practical, and we didn't believe in trusting people outside of the household. But no matter what happened, I still had this deep down belief that I could make things better, and I had this kid, and I knew that I wanted him to have a better relationship with life than I had. I was always fighting and pressing. The world had become more of an obstacle course for me, but I wanted my son to see opportunity first, not the obstacles that lay before the opportunity. I wanted him to see possibility, and I couldn't make that happen if I didn't make a change. I had grown up in discord, and I didn't have the skills to negotiate marriage, but I did not want my son to have to be a victim of my problems.

I felt guilty for choosing my son over the marriage, and I think in many ways, that guilt kept me from being as assertive as I would have been had I been whole and guilt free. Abuse, rancor, and confusion in a household inseminate self-doubt, low self-esteem, self-hatred, fear, depression, sadness, loss, delirium- there's no way to escape those results. And most times, because that lifestyle is so commonplace, so normal, not feeling the chaotic results of that lifestyle is what seems foreign. And that was my experience. When I thought of leaving the marriage behind, it was as if I would be taking the first steps towards leaving that lifestyle behind for good. And there was some guilt about that. There was this question as to whether or not I deserved that sort of happiness.

So, yes, I was reeling. My whole life, I wanted nothing but the perfection of the Clevers, the wholeness of the Cosbys, the unity of the Keatons; I wanted family; I wanted love. No matter what happened to me, though, no matter whether I got those things or not, I was intent on making sure that my son had what he needed.

The divorce ushered in a new era filled with ugly emails, threats of kidnap, child-custody and visitation fights- all the ugly stuff that happens when adults fight over kids.

My son took the separation from his father much worse than I had thought. I thought that if I left at the early age of two, then my son wouldn't be as impacted. I didn't think that he would even remember. That wasn't the case. I'll never forget the day he started banging his head against the concrete floor when he heard me talking to his father about not being able to come pick him up for their visit that day. We weren't even arguing, and my son had that negative of a reaction, and still, he was only two. Even three years later when my son was five and I had moved back home closer to my family, I was in a bank standing in line while my son was sitting in the children's area with two kids who were probably three to four years older than he. Through the glass partition and across the steel floor, my son's voice floated towards my ear. I heard my son telling them how his mother and father were divorced. He was angry, and he was telling those children about details that I had no idea of how he remembered. My heart sank. He remembered, and he was in pain.

Will I See the Light?

The custody issues and the fighting became too much, and so I moved back home. That move back home seemed catastrophic. The mother my son knew didn't exist anymore. I was torn between loyalty to my family and loyalty to him.

It's amazing. If you had asked me then if I were okay, I would have said that I was fine. Truth was that I wasn't. When I was a young kid, my father had difficulty keeping a job. I think in the back of my mind, I feared the same thing for me. We grew up being taught that the *Bible* was completely true, and there was this strange emphasis on ideas such as there was a generational curse on our family, that the sins of the father continued to future generations, and at that time, those beliefs were always in the back of my mind. I was really fighting hard to create a better life for my son, but every time I had a setback, I felt like those scriptures were true, that my plight was my father's plight, that I was destined, fated to experience the same failures.

I was the first of my siblings to finish college. I had a bachelor's degree in English, but I didn't think that I could get a stable job as a teacher. I didn't think that I would get hired. I just never had the courage to walk into life's front door; I had to use the side entrance.

So, I applied to sell insurance and then to work as an alternative school teacher. I got the job selling insurance, but my son and I came down with a horrible case of strep, and my new company had a strict attendance policy that impacted the money you could make if you missed work within your probationary period. Then I got the job teaching in alternative school. The job was tough, but I had a decent salary. I decided that I would save money to buy a home, and against my better judgment moved in with my parents. So many people I knew always talked about how their parents helped them establish their future. My senior year in high school, I worked two jobs to buy my own clothes and to keep my mom and brothers with food and nice things. I'll never forget when I filed my tax return that year, my dad was bragging that I made half of his income. I wanted to create that familial support that I had been missing my whole life, so I moved in.

One thing I have learned from counseling and experience is to find a way to be truthful without being vindictive, so without dredging up details, I'll just say that the violence that began in my siblings' and my childhood didn't stop just because our age increased. My father has made amends to me for his behavior, and he has suffered plenty for his behavior when we were young. He and my mother have helped me tremendously in recent years. But what my father didn't consider when we were young was that angry, abused little kids turn into angrier, revenge-seeking adults.

Suffice to say that violence entered that household, and I was in a position where I had to either stay and risk the threat of serious violence, or I had to find somewhere else to go. Still trying to save money, I moved in with another family member, and that arrangement was bad in other ways. I came to the point in my life where I realized that if I didn't permanently extricate myself from my family and accept that I could not create the familial support that I witnessed in other families, I would lose my mind, and I would never be able to establish permanence in any facet of my life if I depended on them to create it.

If you notice, my son isn't the focal point of this section of our story. And that's why so many women are willing to stay in a bad marriage- the alternative feels like hell at the time. I was so busy trying to make a living for my son that I didn't have time to nurture the relationship with him, yet I had gotten out of the marriage in the first place so that my son would not suffer.

During this time, my only focus was to get us financially stable and out of harm's way. So I was robotically going through the motions in buffer mode. I was trying to make enough money to create a nice, stable home for him. I never stopped taking him to the park, buying him toys, taking him to museums, putting him in fun programs; I did all of that, but I was always trying to make sure that he said the right things and behaved perfectly. I didn't want him to have any traumatic experiences with my family members or anybody else. That was a really hard thing to do because the more he began to talk, the more I started to hear that his interpretation of whatever was going on was just off. He sounded so intelligent, but the longer he talked, the more I could hear him veer off into some other concept related to something he must have been thinking about. It was usually about his Thomas toys, but sometimes, those conversations turned angry, and I didn't know why. And I, "Ms. Fix It", was just trying to always be there to make sure I could turn the conversation to make him look "normal".

It was probably some time in February when I got the idea to move away. I was only legally allowed to live in my home state as a condition of the custody agreement, so my options were limited. Then one day after I got my tax return, I decided that my son and I would go visit

Northern Virginia. We drove up one night, found a hotel and stayed right on King Street just near the Metro. I had never been on the Metro in DC. I had gone to visit a girlfriend in New York only once, so I had one experience with the subway. But I had always dreamed of living in a big city. I'm the artsy type; as a little girl, I loved Sesame Street and wanted to go live in the city just as they did. I love museums and art galleries and edifices that mark time and place. I love history and sitting within the memory of a space. There is magic in that.

I remember getting to Northern Virginia with no plan at all. I hadn't even thought of booking a room until I got there. I called some hotels in Crystal City, and I remember them telling me that I couldn't even book the room without a credit card. I didn't have a credit card; I had cash, so I drove around and called around looking for a hotel that accepted cash. We finally found one on King Street as I said. We went to a Target to find some food that we could nibble on at the hotel. And I remember going into a fast-food restaurant and seeing my basketball coach hero John Thompson. He must have seen me looking without trying to stare. He spoke to me. I was in shock! I remember feeling like I was in time, my "supposed to be" time. I remember getting back to the hotel and laying my son down in that luxurious bed. He looked so peaceful, so small, but so content. He was safe. I remember starting my plan, doing the research- no time for rest for me- planning, just planning. I remember turning on the news looking at the newscasters, analyzing the way the newscasters talked, and trying to figure out what made people tick in that area- I would need to be able to speak their language if I were going to be able to get a good job and make a good living for us.

When we left the next day, I knew that we were coming back. I didn't know how, but I knew that we were going to come back to live. It seemed far-fetched for me- the poor daughter of a preacher; the girl who always sounded like an intelligent person but felt like a dummy, afraid that any day people would find out her truth; the girl who felt like she knew nothing of love; the girl who always felt out of place. But that girl's fears weren't louder than the love I had for my son. That kid had made me love pink; there was no telling what else he could get me to do.

New Life

I was in a place where I knew that if I didn't take drastic steps to save my life, I would not be around to live it. I was literally suffocating in my own thoughts, and I had to move, take steps, do something to find a better way. So one day, after finding some information about a program in Northern Virginia that helped women who were having struggles like mine, I packed every belonging I had into my car and set off to find my new future.

Kind of Blue took me up to Northern Virginia on that day in April, and it brought me back. As I sit here now, I can't imagine driving a couple hundred miles to some place I'd never been. I can't imagine not calling them. I don't remember what I was thinking; I just knew that the way I had lived all of my life wasn't something that I could continue.

My son thought we were on another adventure. We spent the first night at a rest stop. I read books to him, and we played and giggled in the car until he fell asleep. I couldn't sleep. I didn't have a lot of money, my car was old, I didn't know exactly where I was going, I didn't know if my plan would work, if my son's father knew what was going on, I thought he'd use it to fight for custody of my son...

But a couple of years before, my granddaddy was sick in the hospital when I wasn't sure how to get out of the marriage, and I asked him what I should do. In a feeble voice he said, "When you're in the middle of the swamp, the best way to get out is any direction you take." My grandfather had been a major voice of reason for me as I was growing up. Everything he and my grandmother did was to make sure we were taken care of. When they found out that my dad wasn't working, they started buying our groceries. He was a traditional man, however. He was a child of the Depression. Men and women had certain roles. I had been afraid to tell him that I was getting a divorce. I didn't want him to consider me a failure. But when he responded like that, it gave me a lot of courage. That trip to Northern Virginia to try to find another life, another way of thinking- that was my "any direction you take". And I was betting everything I had, including my son's life and every penny I had, on that one chance.

I didn't fall asleep in the car until it was close to morning. I had only been sleep for a couple of hours when the state trooper started driving through the parking lot signaling to folks that it was time to leave. I was so tired. I could not stay awake. I will never forget. I was the last person in the parking lot, and he drove his car about 40 feet away from my car, turned his lights on and sat there until I left. I was so tired. I found another place to park so that I could get myself together.

When I finally got rolling, I followed the directions to the facility. I got there. The parking lot was empty, and the windows were black with some sort of covering. I looked for a door, I listened for people's voices. Nothing, I heard nothing. I don't remember how it happened, but somebody told me that social services might know where the facility had moved. When I went there, I was told that I needed to go back home. They couldn't help me because I was a resident of another city. They had no idea where the women's program had moved, but they couldn't help me. In shock and hoping I had enough gas money, I drove those couple hundred miles back. I had been told to call the National Domestic Violence Hotline. When I got back home, I did. I used the telephone in the lobby of the social services building in my city, and I broke down crying. They put me in touch with a local women's shelter for women experiencing domestic violence. The woman I spoke to arranged for me to meet her at a safe place, and then I followed her with all of my belongings piled high in the car with only one small space in the back carved out for my son and his car seat.

I stayed between that facility and another that helped me find permanent housing for about six months, and I attended mandatory domestic violence group sessions where people talked about survival. I told my son that the first facility was a hotel, and he called the other facility "a house with rooms". He was able to attend art therapy and receive toys and food and a birthday party and structure while I was trying to get our lives on track. Those six months changed my life. For the first time, I realized that there were people outside of my family who would help me, that abuse and rut-living wasn't a destiny but choice. I learned that happy endings did exist. And I learned how to set limits to protect myself and my son from unnecessary trauma. I learned to be able to communicate better. I learned that the statement that hurt people hurt people is true and that I could learn to work on relationships with the people in my family who genuinely wanted to work on them with me. Most importantly, I learned that I had the right to prioritize my son and his wellbeing.

Finally, after a year or so, I started teaching. Things didn't go so well the first year, and then I got a job as a writing specialist in another district. It was that position that ushered in the permanent stability that I needed to be completely headed in the right direction. I worked hard, made a good name for myself, and after two years decided that I would make that move back up to Northern Virginia. It took a little time, but I got my dream position- a twelfth-grade English teacher in a very nice district. My son was attending school in one of the highest ranked school systems in the country, and we were well on our way to lifelong success. What could go wrong? Despite every obstacle we'd faced, we had made it.

See, He's Different

My son's first encounter with education outside of our home occurred when he started daycare on my college's campus when he was two years old. At home, I had taught him the fundamentals. By about four, I had taught him to read. I really emphasized education, so his delays were not related to academics as much as they were related to social development.

We were attending a research-focused university, and so all of the practices at the daycare center were based on the newest research available. His teacher called his father and me in one day to observe him. She said that he did some things "differently" when compared to the other children. There was an observation room in the center of the facility, and they brought us inside being careful not to allow my son to see us. I remember standing inside of the room and watching him and not really seeing what she was talking about. At home, my son always loved to have playmates around, he just never played with them. He was always off doing his own thing, but he liked for the children to be around. I thought that that was just because he was an only child. I probably agreed with what the woman was saying to her face, but I never really saw it. I thought that he was too young for us to label him as being different; I thought that whatever made him different, I could eventually teach him to correct. More than anything, I was too nervous to hear her. My stomach was always in knots. I pretended to be strong; I was a forceful advocate for my son, but inside, I was a complete ball of knots. I just didn't want to have one more thing wrong until I could graduate and get us on our feet.

Fast forward a few years, and the same observations were being made about my son from the time he entered kindergarten through fourth grade. School was really tough for him. As a teacher, I have never really understood why all of his elementary school teachers required him to copy the day's agenda from the board, but they did, and it always took him hours to complete it.

It was excruciating for him, but at the time, I did not know why that simple writing task was so difficult.

He also had horrible experiences with being physically attacked in first grade. He had major difficulty reading facial expressions and recognizing social cues. I was constantly in contact with his teachers about problems he was having with other students. It was so hard. The problems were real to him. I just could not understand why kids being kids bothered him so much and why those misunderstandings led to such drastic and negative interactions, sometimes physical, more often verbal. Academically, however, he excelled, until the first part of third grade. All I could think of during that time was that I had to work and he had to attend school, but in all honesty, we were flailing around in the deep end of the pool.

Besides the time when a family member joked that my son was autistic, I had never considered that he might be. I had taught autistic children when I worked for the alternative school, and my son just did not present with that level of functioning. But when you're a teacher, the truth is that you can be thrown into a class like that and never thoroughly be trained in that area. I researched some things about autism, but I certainly did not have enough information, and it is amazing to think of how inept I was about Asperger Syndrome. To my way of thinking at the time, my son wasn't anything like the character in *Rain Main* who had some extraordinary ability; my son was very smart, like at age two he could name every car that he passed by looking at the symbol, but by the time he was four, he had forgotten all about car emblems. More than that, he liked to be around other children. Even though he never played with the children when they were around, everything I had heard about autistic people suggested that they didn't like to be around other people. And even more than that, I had never heard of aggression and anger being associated with autistic people. My son would react potently. I thought that kids with autism didn't register emotion. My son overly registered it. To top it off, no teacher suggested that he might be on the autism spectrum. Because I advocated for him so strongly, teachers tended to act as if my son were just bad or spoiled. But I knew how my son behaved at home and with anybody who watched him. He never talked back, he did what he was told, he followed instructions completely. It was just when he got to school around lots of other people, something happened. He changed. He was anxious. This was a kid who could play with Thomas train sets all day without interruption except to get something to eat. Nobody ever minded taking my son with them; they actually enjoyed it because they would learn something from him, even though he was a young child, and he was really, really sweet and pleasant.

By around second grade, a friend of mine told me about a doctor who tested kids for ADHD. I took my son to see him, and he was diagnosed. I thought I had found the answer. I took this diagnosis with me when we moved to Northern Virginia and expected that this knowledge would help make things better for him in school. But things didn't get better at all; things went haywire. What I've learned since that time is that the academic demand for more abstract thinking really increases between the second and third grade school years, and these skills tend to be highly problematic for children on the autism spectrum. Given that transition, it makes sense that my son's issues manifested as dramatically as they did. That compounded with the fact that we had just moved rattled his world.

Without an adequate diagnosis there was no treatment, and without treatment, my son had become outwardly aggressive. He had both perceived and actually experienced so much mistreatment throughout his time at school that he had decided to become the aggressor to avoid further pain. In third grade, he was almost expelled from the school system because he verbally threatened some kids who were laughing at him on the bus. They were laughing at him because he had put his book bag over his head to try to block out the bus noise, and some crumbs from his book bag had fallen on his head. For two months while we were awaiting the expulsion hearing, my cousin was able to keep my son for me and help him keep up with his schoolwork. She had taught autistic children as well. At the same time that

I was awaiting the expulsion hearing, I was going through the special education eligibility process for my son, and when we got to the section that evaluated for autism-related behavioral patterns, my cousin helped me see some of the behaviors that I had missed. She helped me realize how he whirled around randomly, how he was so precise with his language, like a professor or something. He was also sensitive to noises but only sometimes. My son's characteristics were so smorgasbord to me that I did not recognize them as clear indicators of any one specific disorder. But because she wasn't so used to his behaviors, she recognized them as symptomatic of a larger problem.

By a narrow margin, he was not expelled from the school system, and he was approved for special education services. I took him to a neurologist and got the diagnosis, and I was able to get him placed in a school that focused on kids with autism. However, even though I did get the diagnosis of Asperger Syndrome, I didn't know what that really meant. I didn't know how deeply it impacted his ability to process the mounds of information that people receive and are expected to use in a given day. I only understood that Asperger Syndrome needed to be worked around, not considered. So between third and fourth grade, I really worked to make sure that he ended that outwardly aggressive behavior. What I didn't know then was that because I wasn't treating the autism/Asperger Syndrome, because I wasn't talking to him with the understanding of how the autism/Asperger Syndrome shaped his particular way of thinking, I was making the problem worse. I thought that my son's problem was that he was being outwardly aggressive when he misunderstood other children's behavior. What was actually going on was that he felt like something was wrong within himself when he didn't understand other children's behavior. I was tired of him being suspended, and I told him so. I was tired of the negative impact his behavior had on my ability to work, and I told him so. But because I did not realize how much pain he was in, I pushed the idea that the outward aggression needed to stop. And so it did, until I realized that he simply changed the outward aggression to inward aggression, and he just decided that everything would be better if he did not exist.

I had had thyroid surgery, and so I was home recovering when my son came home from school one day and said that he wanted to kill himself. I didn't know what to do. Every day felt like a crisis. And as a parent, I have to say that because I felt like we were always in crisis, I didn't know how to skillfully process what to deal with first. I thought he was venting angrily. I talked to him about it, but like every other problem he faced at school, it felt like I was putting a bandage over a gaping hole; but I did not know what else to do except talk to him and contact the school and continue to seek medical advice. I just wasn't really sure of how serious he was.

It just so happened that I was watching the *Oprah* show the next day, and the guest was discussing the issues that led her son to commit suicide. Some short time later, the woman came on the *Ellen* show. Because I was seeing her for the second time, I paid more attention, and I distinctly remember someone saying that if your child mentions committing suicide, to ask them if they have a plan. When my son came home that day, we talked about his day, and I gently brought up the conversation about him wanting to harm himself. I found a way to ask him how he would do it, and to my surprise, he had a complete, detailed plan. To say that I was in shock would be the understatement of the century. It threw me into an entirely different realm of existence. I already had an IEP phone conference scheduled, and I told his school team what he had told me. One of his counselors burst into tears and told me to hide every item in the house that he was planning to use. She had had a family member that had actually gone through with a plan.

I was sick to my stomach and scared beyond reason, but I never let my son know how I felt. I just started making decisions- I wasn't going to let my son harm himself. There were only a couple of weeks left in the school year, so I told the school that I would be keeping him home and that I would be preparing him for his end-of-year exams. Much to their behests, that is exactly what I did. I knew that I needed guidance, more than I already had, but I didn't know where to get it. I could not send him back to school until I could figure out how to help him.

Homeschool: Is This Really Going to Happen?

When I talked to my mom about the situation, she was ready to come live with us. Even though I hoped she could come, I didn't think she was going to be able to. For most of that summer, I tried to determine whether or not I really was going to do homeschool. How was I going to pay rent, how was I going to feed us? I had the job that I had been trying to get since I had begun considering the move to Northern Virginia. Was I really going to have to quit?

But the issue on the other side of the scale was outweighing everything I could think of. July and August went by quickly, and my mother couldn't come as I'd thought. My grandmother had become really ill. My father ended up having a mini stroke not long after that.

I contacted my supervisors and quit my job. I knew that I couldn't send my son back to school. His IEP contained every support available: social skills training with social scripts, extended time, time outs, counseling support, pull-out as needed; there were no other supports to try, and my son's progress was deteriorating. I had to intervene.

I didn't know how I was going to do it. But every time I walked out of my bedroom, I had to pass my son's room, and nothing that I felt trumped the fact that that kid needed to be taken care of. And that meant that I needed to get my act together quickly and get homeschool running while I tried to find every resource possible to help me get him on track so that he could go to school and I could go back to work.

Every day I had to fight fear. I had made the toughest decision I had ever made in my life. I knew that I had to take care of my son, but how in the world was I going to keep a roof over his head? I knew that I had to take care of my son, but I did not know if I had made the right decision to homeschool a child who already lacked social skills. I knew I had to take care of my son, but how did I know that my plan would work?

I placed myself on autopilot, and I just went through the motions so that no matter how afraid I was or how worried I was, I just kept moving towards my goal to make sure my son was okay.

As you will see in the next few chapters, I developed a plan to help my son. But I want to be clear- this plan didn't just happen. I had to get over being afraid, I had to seriously determine if what I was doing was the right thing for my son, and then I had to be strong enough to keep working on my plan when people doubted me.

I wondered how in the world I was going to be able to get my son to function in this world. Human beings are already socially nervous. It's a part of who we are. We are all constantly volleying within social environments to be heard, to be accepted, and to be understood. We understand what it means to feel rejected, ostracized, and misunderstood. I think that that is one of the reasons why rearing the autistic child can be so difficult. None of us are complete social experts. So it is hard to teach a child how to socially interact with the world when that child has limited inclinations about social behavior, and we struggle with it ourselves. Our rules are always shifting and adjusting, and the way we socially interact with the world is largely based in the way we perceive ourselves, whether that be positive or negative. Our insecurities, our fears, our strengths, everything we are goes into the way we interact socially, and most of the time, these interactions occur so swiftly and are so commonplace that we do not analyze them, we don't think about them too critically, so when we need to explain these nuances to our autistic children, we are at a loss.

Within autism's presence, I stopped trying to be perfect. I found that I could be truthful with my son about how difficult I found it to interact with people, and that took a lot of pressure off of both him and me. I learned that it was okay, normal to make mistakes.

We did not have to be perfect, but we did have to have some ground rules. I had to stop trying to make the world seem like a nice little fairy tale, like he had seen on TV. I had always been so protective, but I realized that he needed explanation and that explanation crafted in a child-appropriate way was necessary. I had become so "busy" that I had stopped having those necessary conversations that I had had with him when he was much younger. I realized that I had to have enough confidence in truth to talk to him about complicated issues that impacted the way he needed to communicate. I had to be able to talk to him about bullying and why some kids behaved as they did. I had to talk to him about racism and prejudices that people have against difference. I had to talk to him about the prejudices people held about people with disabilities, and I had the difficult task of trying to get him to appreciate himself, autism and all.

I had to develop the ability to be patient with myself. I realized that I needed that same patience for my son and that I needed to help him cultivate that same patience for himself. I realized that the pressures I had placed on myself to be successful were just my attempt to be seen by the world as accomplished and acceptable. I wasn't doing the things that I had always wanted to do with my life. I was doing what provided me with that perceived stability. I realized that I wanted to look "normal" and to be the stability that I had wanted as a child.

But, I had a child with autism, and he needed me to be the parent who let him be himself. He needed a parent who didn't need him to be perfect. He needed a parent who had time to hear him. He needed a parent who would take the time to understand him. He needed a parent who wouldn't try to make him fit into a schedule that did not take his unique abilities into consideration. He needed a parent who would value his unique presence. He needed a parent who was not consumed by the need to be better than her childhood experiences. He needed a mother who was malleable herself, open to his way of thinking, still courageous enough to challenge him lovingly so that he could see alternative perspectives. I had to learn to adjust to be the sort of parent that my son needed to get him to create his own goals and to find his level of fulfillment.

I was scared, nervous, and insecure, but I didn't have an alternative. I had to get my son to a level where he could function in this world. While I had been in my classroom teaching children with and without special needs, and some of them even had autism, my phone would be vibrating in my pocket, and it would be my son's school calling to tell me that he was in some sort of trouble. I had to do it. No matter how I felt, I had to find a way to get my son to some positive level of functioning. And so, as difficult as it seemed, we embarked on our process.

Part Two

Homeschool and Our Strategies

Navigating Human Interactions and Expressions

There were a few memories that guided the decisions that I made while I homeschooled my son. One, of course, was the reason that I had begun homeschool in the first place. Another was an incident, which took place towards the end of my son's second grade school year. I was picking him up from school early, and his class was standing in line getting ready to head back to the classroom. His classmates started to tell him goodbye; they were waving and smiling, and my son turned around angrily and said that none of them were invited to his birthday party. The hallway noise quieted my son's response because when I looked at the kids' faces, it didn't seem that they heard him. But that behavior wasn't anomalous. If he had been angry enough to behave that way in front of me, then I knew that he truly believed that the children did not like him, even though I could clearly see that they did. And I knew that there were times when loud hallway noises were not present to keep my son from being heard, and this impacted his ability to form quality relationships with other children.

Over time as I began to put the pieces together, as I began to recognize those behaviors that were characteristic of Asperger's, I realized that my son had a huge problem discerning normal interactions between people. He had been so hurt by the kids who had bullied him that he just lumped all kids into the same category because that was the safest decision that he could make for himself. He did not have the ability to tell whether or not someone was genuinely nice, so if he treated everybody as if they were a threat, then nobody could hurt him. So during homeschool, I knew that I was going to have to teach my son how to determine standard human behavior and human expression.

In homeschool, another quest was to try to help my son find balance. I wanted him to be able to understand how to self-manage and self-regulate so that no matter the situation he might be in (bullying; not being sure if someone was really being his friend; trying to explain his perspective when others disagreed, yet he knew that he was accurate) he wouldn't resort to aggression. I wanted him to develop the calm within which he needed to exist in order to navigate the environments he occupied at any given time. He needed the self-confidence and flexibility to not need people to agree with his opinion. Quite frankly, I had to help him see that sometimes people would disagree with him not because they really did but to get him frustrated. And I had to show him that that sort of behavior didn't have to mean that the person was always good or always bad, but that that behavior should be a guide to be used to determine whether or not he would want to spend time with or entrust that person with important information. I had to teach him how to navigate the world socially, and I had to do so in a way that didn't cause him to parrot all of my social behaviors. I had to give him a clearer set of social standards that he could use to make his own choices about how he would be perceived and understood within the environments he occupied.

What was already in place: He was used to me talking to him. We had a clear routine and clear rules and expectations.

Obstacles:

- He was used to me talking to him, not necessarily listening to him.
- He did not really trust me.
- He didn't know me.
- He thought he was smarter than I was, and he didn't really believe me when I was teaching him.
- He was still angry.
- I didn't know how we were going to finance homeschool, so it was really hard to focus on these goals when I wasn't sure how I was going to meet our basic needs.
- Because my son wasn't diagnosed with an autism spectrum disorder until he was eight years old, we didn't deal with him before that time as if he had a disorder that would impact the decisions

that we made in regards to his care. As a result, over the summers when he visited his dad, he looked at a lot of the television shows that kids watch. But what happened was that my son began to seriously base a lot of his understanding about how people interacted with each other on the way people behaved in the TV shows that he had watched. I needed to help him develop a more realistic understanding of how people dealt with one another.

How we worked on it:

I wanted to show my son how people interacted with each other, so I printed a copy of labeled facial expressions and discussed them with him. We focused on looking at the nuanced differences. For example, we analyzed the difference between frustrated and sad. We talked a lot about the differences and the consequences of misunderstanding expressions. I modeled facial expressions for him. We looked in the mirror together to help him emulate and interpret the facial expressions and to adjust the body's movement to reveal the sentiment of the expression. I taught him not to jump to conclusions about the meaning of a person's facial expression but to ask more questions to determine the other person's mood, feeling, or intent. I taught him to try to analyze body movement to determine feeling. For example, to determine the difference between frustrated or sad, I told him to ask what happened and listen to the mood or feeling the person expressed; I told him to watch the person's body language to help determine mood. And I had to teach him to recognize basic body language like shrugging shoulders, patting feet, fidgeting, and nodding heads. I would take him to public places like museums or restaurants where we could sit inconspicuously and watch people interacting. He didn't know that that was my design. We would be on an outing, and I would watch for examples of interactions that I could show him.

I remember the first day I did this. We had gone to the Natural History Museum to supplement something we were learning in science. I noticed this family, and one of the couples in the group was having a disagreement, but they were doing so discreetly. My son and I sat down and, without being obvious, I showed him how they were whispering. I told him to look at their facial expressions so that he could see what anger and frustration could look like on faces other than mine and his. I asked him how he would feel if they were outwardly aggressive and loud in the museum. I asked him how he thought others might feel if the couple were arguing loudly. And I asked him how he and the other patrons benefited from the couple masking their anger.

We did this sort of thing almost every time we went out, but I never set it as a goal for the adventure. The goal was always the fun place we were going to visit or the new place where we were going to eat. Every outing became an opportunity to talk to him about why positive social interactions were important and to show him what expression looked like in a variety of human beings. But, I was always careful to do this when my son wasn't occupied with something that was really important to him. If I made the observation the goal, then it would have seemed like a chore. I wanted him to learn it as just a way of doing things.

Eventually, we got to the point where we discussed whether or not that behavior masking, like the couple had done to avoid displaying their disagreement, meant that my son was betraying or lying about his true feelings. That was a big issue because I had to help him explore those nuanced differences, those fine lines between lying about his feelings and making a concerted effort to display his feelings in a way that allowed him to get his point across but didn't cause him to be perceived negatively because his behavior did not negatively impact other people around him.

One good thing about living in a city and riding buses and the subway is that you are guaranteed to find someone behaving badly and making the other passengers feel uncomfortable. Well, I know it's not really a good thing, but God bless everybody who made my son feel uncomfortable on those trips because those instances allowed him to build empathy for people who might have felt uncomfortable as a result of his behavior when he became frustrated. In no way did I dismiss the relevance of the cause of his past outbursts; I wanted to make sure that he understood why it would be a good idea to express the anger in a better way. And so I would model for him how to deal with negative situations positively. I would use simple situations like having to return damaged goods. I would take the item back to the store and tell my son to watch the way I interacted with the salesperson to negotiate restitution for my problem. Any time there was a conflict, I would talk to my son about the best way to handle it, always appealing to his logic and showing him the benefit of choosing the response that would reap the result he was looking for.

Even when we looked at images of the war on the news, we talked about how the soldiers had to behave aggressively in combat situations to save their own lives and the lives of others, but then I showed him how stressful it was for soldiers to live that way, and we talked about the impact of that required behavior on their long term health. And then, I had to help him see how his behavior impacted his own health and mental well-being. I had to talk to him about how he needed to choose to make decisions that would allow him to enjoy life in the way that he really wanted to.

I also wanted him to see how people displayed love and affection. He was used to me meeting his needs, but I had not taught him to be thankful and gracious when I gave him things. I had taught him to say "please", "thank you", and the like, but I didn't realize that he made those statements robotically out of the need to follow my instruction, not as an emotional expression of his feelings. Also, I never wanted to make my son feel like he owed me anything. For whatever reason, I always felt like my job was to take care of him, not the other way around. So, I had to learn how to get him to really understand why ideas like love and gratefulness were important. For example, whenever we would go into the city, we would always see homeless people. I would talk to him to try to get him to imagine what it would feel like if he did not have anyone to care for him. I tried to teach him to imagine his life if he did not have his toys and the other things that he had that made his life joyful. I tried to make sure that he had all of the things that he really wanted so that he would feel some sense of satisfaction. We didn't buy everything he wanted, but I talked with him to help him determine what he really wanted, and I made sure I found a way to get him those things. And so because he felt fulfillment, he was able to imagine what it would feel like if he didn't.

In the same way, I wanted him to see that his life was important because he could use his fulfillment to help others. We started volunteering for different causes, and it really helped him feel like he had a valuable part to play in our society. Building on helping others, he loved to hold the door open for people. Even when people didn't say thank you to him, I made sure I told him how nice it was that he was trying to help people.

I also made sure that I taught him that there was a difference between helping someone and being used. I had to help him see the gray areas involved in both his own behavior and interpreting the behavior of others. I tried to make sure that he understood that it was more than okay for him to be protective when he was not sure of another person's motives. We weren't rich, so when we passed people on the street who were asking for money, we discussed whether or not we had the ability. We discussed whether or not we should give away our resources when we weren't sure how the other person might use them. I didn't shy away from those conversations because I knew that he needed to be comfortable protecting himself in healthy, thoughtful ways. I knew how angry he became when he found out that someone had tricked him, and I wanted him to know that calm, healthy skepticism was okay. I taught him that when he went to school, he didn't need to get angry when he suspected someone of taking advantage of him. I taught him to be calm first and then to ask questions. I made sure that I would talk to him about the questionable interactions he would have, and I made sure that when I visited his school for programs or when I picked him up from school, I observed as best as possible the students he had referenced so that I could see if I noticed skeptical behavior. Sometimes I did, and other times, I didn't, and we talked about it. The one thing that I tried to do was to teach him that he could be patient with himself and that because he wanted healthy relationships with people, he needed to give himself the time and patience necessary to ask questions and to be comfortable withstanding the pressure kids would put on him to respond to them swiftly. And when it came to whether or not he would give his money to a needy person asking for it, I let him make the decision, and what I found was that he gave the money when he could and wouldn't when he couldn't. I just remember watching him become more comfortable as he started thinking through his decisions and doing so with patience for himself, and I was really happy about that.

In addition, I actually tried to hug and kiss my son more. When he was a baby, I smothered him with hugs and kisses, but when I thought about it, when I moved back home when he was still very young, I was so focused on survival that I was even more physically distant from him. To add to that, the more problems he had in school, the more distant I had become. I realized that I had to show my son more unconditional love. If we had a bad day, I made sure I found a way to bring us back together some way. I intentionally called him in to share in some special food or some game or some funny thing I had found online or on TV. I didn't want my reaction to him to be punitive. I wanted to be restorative. I wanted him to know that we could work together to fix things; mistakes were okay but required repair. I made sure that I no longer made him feel bad about himself. I made mistakes, he made mistakes, but we both loved each other, and we could both come together to solve our problems and try to be the best version of ourselves that we could be. And so, I really made the effort to put my arm around his shoulder, to pat him on the back, to spontaneously tuck him in bed with lots of kisses, all while he laughed and hysterically tried his best to keep any of them from landing. I just made sure that I let him know that I loved him. I had to make sure that he knew that he was special and valuable to me.

Who Am I, and What Am I Worth to Myself and to This World?

Growing up, I didn't live with a great deal of compassion for myself. Somehow, my way of coping with living in a rough home environment was to give myself no excuse for, no pardon for, no justification for moral irresponsibility. I couldn't be what I witnessed at home. I think that I tried to be behaviorally perfect. I didn't give myself any leeway for moral impropriety. Every rule that my mother set had to be followed precisely, and no matter how badly I might disagree, if I could not convince her to change her mind, I obeyed and refused to have a negative attitude. I became rigid. And that didn't change when I became a parent.

When I moved myself and my son back home after college, I was motivated by fear, and I lived in this self-taught rigidity. I didn't want my son to say the wrong things because I didn't want him to be ridiculed. When he and I were on the college campus, I felt much freer to be myself and to allow him to develop without judgment. That freedom to be who we were motivated me to move my son to a larger city. I knew he was like me; I knew we needed a variety of avenues through which to express our personalities. I just hadn't realized how much damage those years at home had done- my entire focus had been on survival.

But human beings are not designed for just survival living. We need self-expression, we need to ask questions, we need to have our questions answered. I had been available to answer my son's intellectual questions, but I lived in denial about the way he processed his world, and I didn't engage in his "different" way of thinking. I masked it. I tried to make it look more acceptable.

So in homeschool, I deliberately chose to let my son be who he was, to deliberately stop trying to make him "normal" to the world. And that meant that I had to begin to accept myself, not the "perfect" person that I was trying to be.

One other belief that guided me in this endeavor was this: When I was in the first women's shelter, I spent every day looking for a job. My son was four, so I would take him with me to do the searches. But on one particular day, I had set up an interview at a temporary employment agency, so one of the older ladies who had become my friend watched my son for me. Everybody kept telling me that I should apply to teach, but after alternative school, I just didn't think that I could do it. I was applying for every sort of job other than teaching. The particular job at the agency was for a secretarial position, but it paid well.

When I got to the agency, I sat down to take the word processing exam, and I forgot everything I had ever known about Microsoft Word. I could not figure out how to do anything. I was mad! I had a degree and couldn't even remember how to use basic computer software.

I failed of course, and I drove all the way back to the shelter yelling and screaming to God, "Are you real? Are you real?" I wanted to know why my life was what it was. I yelled for twenty minutes or so, and when I stopped at the light, which was about two miles from the shelter, I felt the words, "I am real," and I felt calm. I can't say anything other than, I just know I heard it. I stopped crying, drove the rest of the way to the facility, and walked in. I thanked the lady for watching my son, hugged and kissed him, then headed back to my room to get back on the job search. On the way back, I passed a woman using the phone. Knowing that I would need to make some more calls about jobs shortly, I walked back and motioned to her that I would need to use the phone once she finished. She motioned for me to come to her, and I went over hesitantly because I didn't have time for talking. I was trying to get my son and me into a better situation. But something made me go towards her. The woman said, "Here," and gave me the phone. I was skeptical and said, "Hello," with a bit of an attitude. There was a man on the phone, and he asked me my name, and I told him that I didn't give out my personal information. He sounded taken aback by my attitude. He was a bit flustered, but he said that whenever I didn't know what to do or whenever things got rough and confusing to ask God to show me who I am in Him. And he repeated that. He said that whenever I was confused and didn't know which way to turn to ask God to show me who I am in Him. Then he said that that was all, and I gave the phone back to the other woman. And here's how focused I was on getting us to some level of stability; here's how trained I was to be skeptical of people; here's how calloused I was towards life if it didn't have anything to do with obtaining the normalcy and success that I thought my son and I should have- I did not process what he said. I didn't make any connection between what had just happened and the prayer I had prayed in the car. I was on to the next thing. Time was money, and business needed to be handled. I literally gave the phone back with a bit of irritation. I didn't have time for that interruption; but once again, something made me stop and sit down. The woman finished her conversation with the man. When she hung up the phone, I asked her what that was all about. She looked flabbergasted, then she started talking. She said that she had been calling around looking for a good school so that she could finish her nursing program. She said that she was talking to that man about his and his wife's nursing program, and all of a sudden, the man said, "There is a woman coming into your presence who has been questioning whether or not God is real." She said she started looking around the room and then I walked in the door, and her eyes just fell on me.

I couldn't question that. There just was no way to apply rationale to that moment. There were too many anomalies, and ever since that time, I've always prayed, "Lord, show me. Lord, show me who I am in you." And that prayer guided me as I homeschooled my son. It guided me because I was in the same situation as I had been in the shelter. I had put so much focus on what I thought success should look like that I had failed to pay attention to my son' s emotional needs. That is super hard to reconcile. I grew up struggling to have my physical needs met. Maslow's Hierarchy shows that our physical, basic needs need to be met before emotional needs can be considered. And that's how I felt! But life has a way of turning what we think should be on its head. Life was telling me to get our emotional wheelhouse in order first. Because of my son's extreme situation, I didn't have any other choice but to listen and follow.

What I know beyond a shadow of a doubt is that the work that I did and do with my son was and is more spiritual than anything. I had to help my son tap into who he was in spirit, and I had to teach him to love that being and all of the physical manifestations that he brought to this world with him. In short, my goal was to teach him to reconcile his body's abilities with his own hopes and dreams and desires, and I wanted him to learn how to adjust his expectations with the abilities that he had so that he could enjoy what success looked and felt like for him. It became a yielding process for both of us because what I found was that I could not teach him how to do that without learning to do the same for myself. And that moment in the shelter guided this process.

One thing that I always hear from people who take risks to do what they truly believe is right is that the universe rewards that effort. It may take a long time, but eventually, fruit comes from taking positive steps to live the life you were placed on this earth to live. And fruit comes from loving, watering, and nurturing one's self.

Even more so now, I try to teach my son to have compassion towards himself, to be gentle with himself as he lives on the autism spectrum. I try to make sure he lives with balance between being patient with his set of abilities and working as hard as he can to achieve his goals. I say that I emphasize this even more so now because it has taken me so long to get to the point where I am truly understanding what this love for self means. Yes, I am and always have been a staunch advocate for myself, but that doesn't necessarily translate into love for myself. It certainly translates that I want to protect myself from pain, but it doesn't translate into loving myself. I am just now getting to the place wherein I believe in my ability to achieve my dreams. Take this book for instance. I am now at the place where I feel confident enough to write it. I say all of this to emphasize how important it is for us as the parents to have filled tool boxes; whether that means we gather love for ourselves, knowledge, patience with ourselves, or belief in our own abilities regardless of whether or not anyone else does, we have to be complete and balanced if we want our children to be the same- and particularly so when it comes to rearing our children who live on the spectrum. By nature, they mimic, which means what we do, they tend to do more intensely, particularly when we don't think they notice.

What was already in place: He knew that I would advocate for him. He had solid structure and routine in the household.

Obstacles: He didn't feel that he and I were a family. He was used to me being in charge but not really being connected to him. I had to show him that I loved him, but I was so focused on being the provider and the disciplinarian that it was very difficult to show the vulnerable, loving side because I feared that things would fall apart fiscally, and I feared that he would not fear me enough to follow what I was telling him to do, and then how would he get back to school so that I could get back to work?

How we worked on it:

On the first day of school when we had moved to Northern Virginia, one of my son's assignments was to draw a picture of his family. He had sat with the assignment for hours because he said he didn't know who his family was. I really could not believe it. I had no idea how he could be confused about who his family was. Once I learned that he had Asperger's, I realized that he did not see us as a family because his father and I were divorced, and he and I did not look like the families he saw on television. He thought family should be a mom, dad, and kids. Because we weren't that, he could not see us as a family unit, which meant that he did not see us being emotionally connected as those families would be. He literally told me that he did not think that I loved him. After homeschool, I began to see that I was contributing to this problem. I never required him to buy me Christmas presents or Mother's Day gifts or

Valentine's gifts. I never asked him to help me when I was sick. I never wanted him to feel that he needed to take care of me. That was a huge mistake because by presenting myself as a "needless" person, I was actually reinforcing the social disengagement that already comes with Asperger's. I really was distant from him because I was trying to take care of his physical needs. I wasn't showing him that both giving and receiving love makes a human being balanced.

On top of that, there was this look in his eye. He didn't look like he was really aware of the moments he was in. He was always in a thought about one of his focuses, like Thomas the Tank engine or Marvel characters. But there was also an underlying anger and frustration. It was like he was living in the awareness that he wasn't aware of how other people operated; however, he was aware that the way he enjoyed life offended others too often and ostracized them from him. I had seen that look one time before. It happened when I was in the second women's shelter. There was a night counselor who was really nice, and she was in charge one night. Luckily, my son was with his father at that time during his summer visitation. When I talked to her that night, she seemed off. Her words weren't making sense. I was a resident, so I really didn't want to make any accusations, but I definitely thought something was wrong, and it didn't seem like she was inebriated. Some time in the night, the fire alarm went off, and we all went downstairs. She was walking around just talking crazily, but none of the other residents acted like they thought anything was wrong. I was afraid because there were kids in the building. I told the residents that I thought she pulled the alarm. I told the other residents that I would get her out of the building but that they should lock the door. I remember talking to her. Her eyes were not the same. She really was somewhere else. She was talking about her papa, but I will never forget the look in her eyes. She looked like she had experienced so much pain and so many problems that she just snapped. And that's what I felt had happened to my son. He was fine at home with no noise, no threat of confusion, no one to misunderstand him, but when he went to school, he had a window of about two to three hours before he became overwhelmed and got close to snapping.

So my plan for homeschool was to try to bring him back, to teach him that he could experience disappointment without being devastated, and to teach him to learn himself so that he could respect his abilities to the point where he made choices that made him feel comfortable.

1. The first thing I did was to try to open up communication with him. I just slowly began to get used to hearing him and everything he was trying to express. I started listening to him and talking to him for hours. We still do that today. We process his feelings until he can come to some sense of understanding. This can take days because life is a journey. We don't do it in one sitting. He will go to school, I to work, and if the other sees or hears something that reminds us of the discussion we'd been having, we will bring it up and continue the conversation. And I work really hard to be calm so that he feels like he can

tell me whatever he's thinking without judgment from me. It's not a perfect process. I just keep trying. I am human and am completely fallible, so I don't get the conversations right all of the time; I irritate him, he irritates me, but I just keep trying because that's life, and that's what's necessary.

2. I had him replace negative, angry statements with positive, affirming "I am…" statements. I required him to speak those "I am..." statements repeatedly.

   Example: One night, my son was very angry, and I took him in the bathroom and asked him who he wanted to be. I made him look at himself in the mirror so that he was required to look at himself when he made the negative statements. He couldn't make the negative statements when he looked at himself. When I told him to substitute those words with words that were the opposite of the negative words, he began to smile. Instead of saying that he hated someone, he had to say, "I am love." He had become so

84

frustrated with his life and dealing with autism on a daily basis that he had become very negative, and I wanted to change that. I required him to at least engage with positivity in the hopes that it would lead him towards some level of optimism.

Other "I am…" statement examples:

I am goodness.

I am peace.

I am sweetness.

I am my mother's loved child.

I am my father's loved child.

I am the awesome lover of (Lego, Thomas, X-Men, et cetera).

I am creative.

I am joy.

I am loved.

I am valued.

I am appreciated.

I am an important part of this universe, and I have positive purpose here.

3. I began to tell him that he was precious and valuable to me.

4. I tried my best to get into his world by asking him questions about his special interests and listening carefully to his responses. I learned a lot about the way he thought by listening to him, and that opened up avenues for me to use to teach him. I mean, when he knows something about his interest at the time, he knows it. It's awing.

5. I also tried to develop traditions just for us so that he could have a sense of belonging, and I started involving him in taking care of the household. **Example:** In homeschool, we started making sushi to bring in the New Year. I have absolutely no idea how that started, but he loved it. He's not interested in it anymore, but that tradition went a long way towards helping him realize that he had value and place in our family unit. I also started involving him in cooking the turkey for Thanksgiving and preparing the rest of the meal. He had meaningful jobs to do that required his focus and attention. I still do that now because I

also want him to be able to handle life's requirements when I'm not available to help him. The easier thing to do with a child who has a disability is to keep them away from the difficult task, but that is not good. I think that it is so important for the parent or guardian to build in the extra time needed to teach a child to do challenging things, around the house and in other environments, that are meaningful and require careful attention. And yes, I still struggle with this and have to catch myself doing something that I should be showing my son how to do. His involvement not only fosters responsibility, but it also helps him to feel like he is a vital part of our family unit. For example, the other day, the plumbers came to the house. I got up to meet them while my son was still in bed. I caught myself and called my son down and told him to be available to answer questions or move things, etc. for the plumber. Now of course, I positioned myself so that I would be within earshot of the plumber's questions, but my son didn't know that. He had been assigned the role of being in charge, and with every successful experience kids have with handling new and challenging situations, their confidence builds, and they define themselves as successful and accomplished in that moment.

Now, if for some reason my son fails at a task, we troubleshoot how to do better the next time. And if the failure happened because he didn't listen to or follow instructions, I tell him so. Failure to listen can cause huge problems in the long run, so I address that. Regardless, I always try to find something positive about his performance. It goes a long way towards helping him build his self-esteem.

6. I tried to teach my son to respect his diagnosis. This has been a very difficult task. I know that some parents don't tell their child if they have a diagnosis. I'm not going to suggest whether a parent should or shouldn't, but the belief that guides me is that you cannot make a repair if you

don't know that something needs to be fixed. My son's response to the problems he was having with Asperger's was so drastic that I didn't feel like I had any other choice but to help him understand the role Asperger's plays in the way he processes the world. It has been a constant and persistent push on my end, but I refuse to stop teaching him to respect and consider both his strengths and problem areas when making choices. I am just starting to see him deal with himself with love, compassion, and understanding. I know that that is a direct result of the respect he has for himself.

I also push him to weigh the difference between ability and plain just not wanting to give max effort. I let him know that I cannot tell the difference between those two choices for him because that takes place internally. I explain to him that truthfully analyzing this difference and behaving accordingly marks the difference between being a responsible adult or an irresponsible adult, and there are fitting consequences for both choices.

More than anything, I tell him that he should not feel guilty or inadequate because he does not function like someone who does not have autism. I try to emphasize that they don't have his special abilities either and that each person has his or her own unique role to play in this world. I try to tell to him to focus on his unique purpose because that is what he is here for, to be himself, his awesome self.

Dealing with a Written Expression Disorder

About a month ago, I learned that my son achieved a perfect score on the state writing exam. Of course, weepy, emotional mom that I am, I cried. But, I genuinely had a reason! This was a kid who upon starting homeschool would sit for hours without being able to generate one sentence in response to a given prompt. I was an English teacher! How could that be?

When I was considering homeschool, one problem that I knew would impact my son's ability to perform well on state-mandated exams was that, given the random nature of the prompt selection process, there was no telling what sort of prompt he would get. I actually looked up the released prompt from the year before we started homeschool, and it stated "It has been said that one of the most important things in life is a good friend. Write about someone you think is a good friend to you."

Because of his significant issue with making friends, my son would not have been able to emotionally handle a prompt like that, and I just imagined how many kids on the autism spectrum got that prompt and had difficulty writing about it.

After seeing our autism specialists and finding out that my son had a written expression disorder, the doctors told me that written expression disorders can be a direct manifestation of autism spectrum disorders, and many times the disorder is compounded with motor skill issues that impact the ability to physically perform the act of writing. That prompt required kids on the spectrum to discuss one of the most painful issues they face on a daily basis, but on top of that psychological trauma, they had to deal with both the physical discomfort of writing it, if their school did not offer the exam on computers and the difficulty writing poses when a written expression disorder is present.

So, I knew that I had to give my son a writing process, I had to teach him to be able to write for different occasions, and I had to teach him that writing could actually give him a powerful voice to shape and construct meaning, no matter what the subject of the given prompt. The great thing was that teaching him how to write actually gave me the ability to teach him flexibility, which was so important.

What was already in place: There are many common writing models that can be used to teach a child writing structure. Because children on the spectrum need some predictability, a writing routine/ structure can help lessen the anxiety they might bring to the writing process.

I also knew my son's likes and dislikes, so I knew that I could use this information to help him understand that writing could be enjoyable.

Obstacles: A written expression disorder.

How we worked on it:

1. The first thing that I did was to talk to my son about and show him different types of writing. We had access to the museums in DC, but quite

honestly, you could pull up www.archives.gov (The National Archives) and www.loc.gov (The Library of Congress) to find images of our nation's most important written documents. I wanted to show my son that writing happens in all disciplines. We read the Declaration of Independence, and we talked about how Thomas Jefferson totally assassinated the King of England's character using words alone. We looked at how written instructions in a science experiment is a form of writing. There was a free newspaper that we would always read on the Metro, and my son loved to go directly to the funnies. I taught him that that was writing. I also had him listen to or look at some of my favorite old school hip-hop artists to analyze the way they crafted language in order to present a message. We did that with other music and movies as well. I tried to expose him to writing as the necessary tool that it is, and I wanted him to see the relevance of the skill of writing.

In short, the one thing to do when a child doesn't like or struggles with a particular field of study is to help him or her establish connection to it, to help him or her establish some stake in understanding the subject.

2. The second thing I did was to teach him to pay attention to exactly what he was supposed to be writing about. Quite simply, I had him to write one clear description, which summarized the writing assignment. This step is really important because writing assignments often include multiple questions. So, a prompt may ask a student to provide all of the steps involved in the process of photosynthesis and explain why each is important. If the student only provides the steps involved in the process, they will probably receive a failing grade because they did not explain why each is important. Another example would be that the student is asked to identify a person who has helped him or her in life and describe how the person helped them. If the student simply writes about the person who

helped, then again, the student would probably receive a failing grade because he or she did not respond to the second part of the prompt, which required the student to describe how the person helped. So it is really important to determine exactly what the writing is going to be about before the writing starts, and I made sure my son knew how to do that.

3. The third step was to give my son a writing model. One really common writing model is the five-paragraph essay. It begins with an introductory paragraph which contains the thesis statement (the sentence that tells the audience what the paper will be about), moves on to include three body paragraphs, which provide detail about, support, or prove the thesis statement, and ends with a concluding paragraph that summarizes the main points made in the essay. The main point here is that children with a written expression disorder need some sort of plan to help them get started. If your child struggles with writing, make sure you contact his

or her teacher and set up some time to have your child work with the teacher to develop a writing plan. Different school systems and different teachers use different writing models at times, but if your child has a diagnosed issue with writing, and you all have found a writing model that works well, you can advocate for your child's ability to use the same writing model no matter whose classroom he or she may happen to be in.

4. The fourth step was to teach my son that he could incorporate his special interests into his essay to prove his point. Boy, did that ever make him happy! Let's say he got that prompt about friendship, and he was anxious about it. I taught him that since it was not a research paper, he could, let's say, use an example of friends in a movie he had seen and use that as a source of inspiration for the paper. Instead of answering the prompt using his own experiences, he could use the example. He just had to incorporate the idea while remaining on topic. I explained to him that writing done for exams and class assignments

were designed to evaluate his ability to write, and unless the prompts required him to provide a truthful account, he had the freedom to be as creative as he'd like without going off topic. I explained to him that his scores on state writing tests helped to determine his placement in future classes, and I helped him to understand that the more he understood his ability to craft the writing in his own way, the more he understood writing as an extremely powerful tool that had been used and still could be used to establish nations, to make people laugh, and to make people believe in an idea, the better he would be able to see writing as a powerful tool for his own self-expression.

5. I did require my son to sit with a prompt for a long time until he was able to figure out how to put all of these pieces together. It was very difficult for him at first. I think that first essay took him a couple of days. I remember allowing that to be the only assignment he worked on until he finished it. But once he broke through all of

his own barriers and embraced the process, he wrote wonderfully. Later on in homeschool, he even began writing his own hilarious political jokes.

Addressing Problems with Motor Skills

Before we decided on homeschool, my son had gotten
into a fight with a kid. The kid was joking on my son
because my son had been the slowest runner during gym
class. Some time before that fight, a teacher assistant
had told my son that the child in the class with autism
was beating him on the track. My son was devastated by
that statement. He never wanted to feel like he was
weak, and I could see that that feeling of inadequacy
contributed to his aggression.

I think that the most important point here is to talk to the
child about the problem areas that both of you notice.
Then, seek medical advice. I took my son to an
occupational therapists, and she said that the exercises
that we had tailored at home to meet his needs had
alleviated his problems. So, it is important to make it a
priority to deal with the physical manifestations of
Asperger's because body image impacts self-esteem.

What was already in place: My son wanted to be fit and stronger, so exercise wasn't a hard sell. I used the tracks at the local high school. I found relatively inexpensive five-pound weights, and I bought him an exercise ball. The local recreational centers offered a variety of courses at cheap prices, and the classes that we chose helped my son remain active. Those classes also provided opportunities for him to be around other kids.

Obstacles: Just as most kids who think their parents are ancient and over the hill, my son wasn't convinced that I could teach him to be fit.

How we worked on it:

1. I bought him an exercise ball, and he sat on that when he played video games. It helped to strengthen his core.
2. I took him to the track and taught him how to run with technique. I had run track when I was younger, so I taught him how to position and hold his arms, how to breathe, and how and where to

place his forefoot and heels depending on the sort of running he was trying to do.

3. I put him in swimming classes.
4. I put him in a fencing course.
5. I taught him to do more calisthenics, like push-ups and sit-ups so that he could use his own body weight to build strength.
6. I taught him to pay attention to the technique of his movement because with Asperger's he tended to overlook details for things that he really wasn't interested in.
7. We jogged and exercised together.
8. I did yoga a lot, and while I didn't make him do it, I exposed him to the breathing techniques so that he could use them to keep him calm when he felt anxious.
9. I tried and still try to give him tasks that require him to use those fine motor skills. Included in that goal was the goal to teach him to hold a pencil or pen in a way that would be comfortable for him. I taught him to be okay with taking a break when his fingers hurt. Playing games like

catch or a silly game like hot potato helped him with coordination. I used to race him a lot until he got so tired of me winning that he figured out how to control his body so that he could beat me.

10. I showed him how to do tasks around the house that required him to use focus like cooking, moving furniture, washing and drying dishes, gardening, cleaning the bathrooms, and keeping his room in order.

11. He was also interested in building and construction, so I bought him a set of simple carving tools and monitored his use of them until he was able to use them safely on his own.

12. I made sure my son had a balanced diet with fresh fruits and vegetables, lots of healthy proteins, lots of healthy grains, and healthy oils. He was very sensitive to vitamins or supplements, so I had to make sure that he got his nutrients from healthy foods. I avoided foods that contained unnatural preservatives, too much salt, and mounds of sugars.

It's always important to seek medical advice when making these sorts of decisions so that you can ensure that you are providing the appropriate types of activities for your child's abilities.

Sensory Issues

Besides some noise sensitivity, which we learned to deal with through self-calming strategies and measures like the use of ear plugs, my son did not have a great deal of problems with sensory issues. However, I think that it is really important for a child to have medical attention if there are problems with his or her speech pattern or if the child has unusual sensitivity to touch or other tactile experiences. Don't allow the child to suffer in silence. Doctors can suggest occupational therapists, audiologists, or other doctors who will be able to help your child.

It is critical to seek help because these doctors can write recommendations to your school so that the school can provide the services or strategies that can make it easier for your child to be able to function in the classroom and access the curriculum.

Keep in mind that when your child has a diagnosed disability, federal law protects your child's right to receive assistive support if the disability impedes/hinders his or her access to learning. Always remember that your government has laws, which support you in your fight to get your child educated. Research the Individuals with Disabilities Education Act (IDEA) and Americans with Disabilities Act for more information.

My own son received speech therapy for a while but progressed out of the program. In many school districts now, students have access to computers for word processing, but if your school does not provide access to computers for word processing and your child has motor-skill issues that impact writing, it's important for your child's doctor to explain that your child will need assistive technology. The school system may have your child evaluated by their therapist, but with a medical doctor's suggestion, it's not likely that a school system will take the legal risk to tell you that they will not comply with a doctor's findings. Bottom line, whether the issue is sensory or anything else, seek medical advice, and get the appropriate supports your child needs to perform well in school.

Seeking the Right Help

The first time I put my son back into school after homeschool, he had in-school counseling support, an in-home counselor, a counselor at a children's hospital, and a strong IEP in a school set up for students who had emotional disorders. He was still having major problems, and I had to pull him out of school for the second time about two months into the school year.

I came to the conclusion that I needed to see autism specialists- not a doctor who could diagnose autism, I needed specialists who were immersed in the old and new research, specialists who could explain specifically how these unique children should be taught and reared. Everything else, I realized, was just a stab in the darkness.

The insurance that I had at the time did not cover the testing that the autism specialists would perform. It was so crazy to me. They were paying for my son to see a counselor at the same hospital that would have done the autism testing, but because many insurances considered autism testing exploratory and not necessary, they would not cover it.

Even though it was frustrating, I kept taking my son to the counselor, and I followed through with her suggestions. Eventually, I found out that a competing insurance did cover the services, so during open enrollment, when I went to cancel the then current insurance and explained why, our case was assigned to a special reviewer.

When you have a child with a disability, documentation is absolutely everything. You can't skip appointments, you can't fail to show up to meetings. If you don't do your part, decisions will be made about your child, and you won't really have a leg to stand on when you don't like the outcome. I say that because any time I needed any sort of service for my son, the first thing requested was documentation. The insurance company was no different. They of course had his medical records, so they could see how many doctors and counselors he had seen and how many tests he had taken, but I was able to provide school records, IEPs, everything to show that we needed help with autism.

They took all of my reports. Some time later, I received a call from my reviewer. Unbeknownst to me, they had taken my son's records to the CEO of the company, and after reviewing his case, the CEO had approved payment for my son's treatment at the autism clinic.

We were placed on the waiting list at the autism clinic, and through a cancellation, we got an appointment with the director of the program. It had taken two years of searching and pushing during homeschool, and I had finally gotten the appointment. When I say that going to that facility changed our lives, I am being extremely literal. They were able to precisely show me how my son's brain processed information. Their report helped me see why he wasn't able to do things that I expected him to do. It showed me his strengths so that I could develop and tailor instructions that allowed him to maximize the use of those strengths. They laid out a clear plan of action for schools to use to develop his IEP. They laid out clear suggestions for me to use at home to support his progress.

Just this summer, we went back to help us develop a plan for adulthood, to help us with stress-management, and to help us manage Asperger's in adolescence.

It's not that a practitioner who does not focus on autism cannot help at all. My experience with autism is that each child is so different that there is no way to use cookie cutter approaches to rearing them. I think that because autism deals with the brains functioning, it's so very important to get the clearest picture of how each child on the spectrum functions. It's like having access to a million dollars but refusing it because you have one thousand. I was putting pressure on my son to do things that he literally could not do without assistance and specific training. And that was detrimental to him. I can't advocate more for children on the autism spectrum to be seen by quality autism specialists.

I did a lot of research before settling on our choice, and most of these facilities have long waiting lists. Get started on your research, and get started as soon as possible. Before scheduling an appointment, I would ask the facility if they develop a diagnostic report, which would include a clear description of the diagnosis, a detailed review of your child's levels of functioning to include executive functioning, social functioning, and academic functioning. If your child has significant sensory issues, I would be sure to ask if the facility makes suggestions in the report about that as well. Be sure to ask if the report includes direct suggestions for the school to use when designing the child's IEP.

I am being so clear about this because I had a parent tell me that she went to a local autism center, and the doctor told her that they did not provide this sort of information. So she had taken her son to a specialist, but the specialist had not been able to provide her with any more information than if she had gone to her primary care physician. Get as much clear support as you can for your child, and take notes about all of your observations so that you can relay them to your child's doctor.

I never felt or feel more normal than when I talk to my son's specialists about autism. If you find the right specialist for you and your child, you are really doing a lot to get you all on the right track.

Routine, the Foundation of Everything

What I know that I did right early on was to establish a consistent routine for my son. Even when we had to move into the women's facility, his bedtime routine and eating schedule did not change. I still took him to fun events. He still had his favorite toys, and he still had adequate time to play with them. Simply put, I have always been very protective of the lengthy amount of time he needs to do both schoolwork and extracurricular activities. Even now, I don't rush him unless it's absolutely necessary because he needs that extra time.

Kids on the spectrum need routine, order, and time to do the things they love and time to process new information. The awesome thing about my son is that once he processes new information, he masters the concept, so now that he is older, I encourage him to build this extra processing time into his schedule as a habit. He has to if he wants to respect his learning abilities and if he wants to feel successful by completing his tasks.

I have read about and heard parents who get really frustrated with their autistic child's need for routine. Parents should seek medical advice if they think that the child's routine needs are so rigid that it interferes with the ability to be flexible and experience life. My own son needed routine because it gave him some level of control. My approach has always been to be the facilitator, to give him parameters within which he could set his own routine but to also insert breaks into his routine so that I could teach him much needed flexibility. For really serious events like medical appointments, school work, etc., I used to plan ahead as much as possible so that my son would have time to mentally prepare for that event. But if I wanted to spontaneously go into the city to work on his schoolwork or to go jogging, he understood my firm rules so well that regardless of whether or not he wanted to go, he went.

Routine goes hand in hand with clear rules and expectations. I did not grow up in a household wherein talking back to adults and having meltdowns because I did not want to follow a rule or instructions was allowed.

That is one thing about my upbringing that I do appreciate. From day one, it was clear to my son that that level of behavior was unacceptable. And setting this expectation didn't require spanking. Having clear, realistic, practical, and consistent consequences for misbehavior works really well. For example, if my son did not follow instructions, computer games were off. And he knew that I was not going to go back on my word. So when I said we had to roll out unexpectedly, he knew that that was what was going to happen. He did not like it, but he did it. But here is the key: barring emergencies, whenever I did this, and I did it often, I would have something really cool planned. I just wouldn't tell him what I had planned because I knew that I wanted to condition him to become more flexible. Unpleasant departure from routine could lead to an exciting day out--- perhaps departure from routine isn't always a bad thing. Planning these sorts of events helped establish that level of flexibility so that when there really was an emergency, my son was better able to handle it.

To be extremely clear, this is no easy task. But you as the parent have to establish routines that work for both you and your children. And if your child happens to take medications, then you definitely have to have a routine for that based on your doctor's instructions.

Imagine a world without routine. Now imagine that your child on the autism spectrum already feels this chaos because autistic children do not connect with the world in the way that people without autism do. And because this is an internal condition, parents and caretakers and people who do not know that the child has autism tend to expect things from these children that the children really can't do. When I learned from our specialists how mentally painful it was for my son to try to process chunks of information that took me seconds to process, I cried. Children on the autism spectrum have serious difficulty trying to follow along, but we judge them sometimes because we can't visually see this struggle. Most of us try to help a person who has a guide dog or a cane. Higher-functioning people with autism can seem like they know more than or as much as we do, so where is the need for help? Why be understanding?

The key word is "seems". Routine helps children on the autism spectrum feel like they have control. Routine is comforting. Routine is reliable unlike facial expressions, which are constantly changing, unlike rules that don't always apply, unlike people's moods, which change within a blink of an eye for reasons that even people without autism spectrum disorders don't always see.

So establish routines, and establish flexibility into your routine. Involve everybody in the household in the process. Don't let drama rule the conversation. Be calm but firm, and you control the conversation in a way that maintains order. Stick to your guns, as long as your decisions are founded and realistic. Be honest about what everybody needs in and from the schedule. Be prepared to troubleshoot. Plans go awry. Be able to have a plan for when the plan doesn't work.

My son was used to this because I always did it. I'm mostly flexible by nature, and I actually enjoy finding alternatives when something doesn't work. However, if you as the parent are not a "turn lemons into lemonade" sort of person, then you and your child can learn together how to come up with creative, satisfying alternatives for your failed plans. It does take work and flexibility. But honestly, when kids see that a second or third plan can reap even better results, it fosters optimism, and kids on the spectrum really need that.

When I homeschooled my son, I always used examples from nature to help him understand my point. Here's a cool one that I didn't even know about when I was trying to teach him flexibility.

Cool example: Most caterpillars can turn into moths within a short while because they are able to feed as much as they need to get pupation started. The wooly bear caterpillar, however, lives in the freezing Arctic, and therefore, its feeding time in the spring is shorter.

Which means, wooly bear caterpillars need another plan to help them turn into moths. They have developed the ability to freeze during the winter, unthaw during the spring so that they can feed, then refreeze again the next winter if they did not feed enough to be able to turn into a moth. If that's not flexibility, I don't know what is! And within that flexibility, there still is clear routine, and in the end, the goal is accomplished. Wooly bear caterpillars can continue this process for quite a few years until they finally become a moth.

Another cool example:

There is one more cool example of an animal that can quickly adjust for survival. It is the cuttlefish! Cuttlefish are actually colorblind, yet their outer layer contains proteins that are normally found in the eye. These proteins allow the cuttlefish to camouflage and become the color of their environment so that they can hide from predators. They also have the ability to make their outer layer become textured so that they can even look like deep sea coral or oddly shaped and colored rock in the ocean.

Use these examples when you talk to your child about establishing and adjusting routines, especially if he or she likes animals or biology. My son and I would even look at stories about famous historical figures who had to develop alternate plans in order to accomplish a mission. Some examples were Harriett Tubman, George Washington (particularly during the Revolutionary War and during the time when he presided over the Constitutional Convention), Abraham Lincoln, and Steve Jobs.

Setting Rules, Goals, and Clear Expectations

Consistency. Consistency. Consistency. Consistency. Consistency.

Consistency. Consistency. Consistency. Consistency. Consistency.

Consistency. Consistency. Consistency. Consistency. Consistency.

Consistency. Consistency. Consistency. Consistency. Consistency.

Consistency. Consistency. Consistency. Consistency. Consistency.

Consistency. Consistency. Consistency. Consistency. Consistency.

Consistency. Consistency. Consistency. Consistency. Consistency.

Consistency. Consistency. Consistency. Consistency. Consistency.

Consistency. Consistency. Consistency. Consistency. Consistency.

Consistency. Consistency. Consistency. Consistency. Consistency.

Consistency. Consistency. Consistency. Consistency. Consistency.

Consistency. Consistency. Consistency. Consistency. Consistency.

Consistency. Consistency. Consistency. Consistency. Consistency.

Consistency. Consistency. Consistency. Consistency. Consistency.

Consistency. Consistency. Consistency. Consistency. Consistency.

Consistency. Consistency. Consistency. Consistency. Consistency.

No, that's not a typo. It really is that important. It really is that vital. Think of it, how often have you ridden by the stop sign in your neighborhood and noticed that the city put up another sign beside it that states "You don't have to obey the stop sign today"?

It doesn't happen. The only time you may be required to ignore that stop sign is if some rare circumstance occurs that makes following the rule impractical. Say for example there is a funeral procession, and you're at the stop sign and the directing police officer tells you to keep moving because he knows the procession will be coming momentarily. In that exceptional moment, you don't have to obey the stop sign. But that is a rare, exceptional moment.

That's how rules should be for children- reliable and consistent. Children know what to expect, so they adjust their behavior and their expectations accordingly.   For kids on the autism spectrum, it's even more important. How do you teach them flexibility when they're not even allowed to have clear consistency?

How would we feel if we were told that Christmas would no longer be December 25th of each year but that from now on, in an effort to control crime, the government would inform us of the date for Christmas with a two-week-in-advance public service announcement?

It's the same way with kids on the spectrum. On one school night, they can stay up playing *World of Warcraft* until 11 p.m., then the next night you get tired of them staying up and so you tell them to go to bed at 9:00, and then you put them on punishment because they have a bad attitude about your decision.

What's my point? We would go absolutely nuts if the government would mandate such a rule about Christmas. In the same way, our kids go absolutely nuts when we change the rules on them mid-game.

As for goals, we all know that goals are important, but goals become extremely difficult to accomplish when consistent rules don't really exist and when there are no clear expectations that support the accomplishment of the goal.

In my own home, much like routines, rules and expectations were firmly in place. What I found, however, was that my son's medical issues kept him from being able to accomplish the goals that we had set. That is why I'm so adamant about getting a clear understanding of your child's diagnosis from an autism specialist who can help you and your child understand which goals are realistically possible. In no way am I saying that the goals must be lessened or less lofty, but understanding functioning will help your child understand the most efficient path that he or she should take to accomplish a goal. So here's what things looked like for me and my son.

What was already in place: Established routines and expectations.

Obstacles: As we have learned more about his abilities, we have had to work through crafting goals appropriately so that they are achievable.

How we worked on it:

1. My son always had a defined bed time and a
    defined daily schedule. Within that schedule, I
    made sure that I planned for the things that he
    needed: favorite toys, food and snacks, and extra
    wipes and diapers when he was a baby. To me, it
    seems easier to implement the routine if the
    routine is pleasant. So for instance, if there is a
    song before bedtime, or if there is breakfast as
    soon as you wake up, or if you can look at a
    favorite show for thirty minutes as soon as you
    wake up, then going to bed isn't so bad. By
    setting up our routine this way, we always had an
    easily consistent regimen. Most importantly, his
    basic needs were always met. When kids have
    their basic needs met (food, shelter, adequate
    clothing, favorite belongings), they are much
    more likely to be agreeable. And when I say basic
    in this sense, I am talking about access to quality
    food and clothing, not necessarily brand name,

but those items that will allow the child to survive healthily.

Now that he is older, my son sets his own routine this way by allotting time for the things that are necessary (school; chores; leisure). Even though he is in charge of his schedule, I can see that the structure is the same as that of his childhood schedule. As he has grown to understand his abilities, he sets his schedule in a way that supports his individual needs. His schedule respects his need for extra time, and he is learning to make decisions about what to include and exclude so that he can manage his time.

2. My son always knew that I expected him to behave respectfully. This has been really helpful as he has gotten older because he realizes that people are more willing to be helpful and tolerant when they are treated with respect. I have also taught him that his reputation is largely based on how he demonstrates respect for people, property, and life in general.

One word of caution, however. Before we really understood my son's diagnosis, my son knew my expectations so well that they were a major catalyst for his frustration. He knew that every time he got into an altercation at school, he wasn't living up to our household expectations. That is why, again, I am so adamant about making sure that you and your child really understand the "why" behind your child's behavior. You can have the clearest routines, the most explicit rules, and the loftiest goals, but if your child has an undiagnosed issue, then you will spend years arguing and pointing fingers and dishing out punishment, the child will feel like a failure, and all of it will have been pointless because the behavior had an underlying issue.

When we started homeschool, we set the goal for me to be able to go back to work and for my son to be able to go back to school. I had my son hang his goal up in his bedroom, but we did not have a clear picture of his diagnosis, so those goals worked as added pressure on him because we did not have a completely clear pathway to obtaining that goal. Once we understood his abilities, we adjusted our expectations to take that pressure off of him, and we found a way to obtain that goal that considered his abilities.

3. Now, in terms of setting up clear expectations, I always used the tenets of a concept in psychology called authoritative parenting. In college, I took a psychology cognate, and I learned about this strategy. I always wanted to be sure to use this parenting style because it is proven to be the most successful. In this style, parents have high expectations for their children, and they make sure that they provide their children with the supports necessary to reach the high expectations. Also, children understand the rules and feel comfortable communicating with their parents about the choices that impact their lives.

Once I realized those areas in which I wasn't really giving my son a chance to express his feelings, those areas in which I really wasn't hearing from him how he felt, I realized that I really wasn't being as authoritative as I had hoped and was, therefore, not reaping the familial benefits of that parenting style.

The truth was that I was afraid to hear how badly my son felt. Instead of hearing him, I was hearing his pain as a negative reflection of how I had reared him. Instead of hearing his issue as a result of the medical condition, I was interpreting it through the ridiculous pressure I had placed on myself to be the perfect mom, the mom who was able to fix and cure everything.

And this is why, again, I say that parents have to have filled tool boxes. I needed the self-confidence and the self-esteem to understand that autism was not my fault. Asperger's was not my fault. My son needed to express whatever he felt through the experience of his particular issue.

Once I understood this, I was able to set clearer expectations for his behavior because he began to talk to me more freely, and I got to be able to understand him better. So now, by having opened up the pathway for him to feel free to communicate, he is as likely to tell me when he may be slacking off as he is when he really is feeling overwhelmed. I am so happy that he talks about the truth of his functionality because I remember what it looked like when he didn't. **Example:** One goal that my son set for himself is to make A's. He knows how his brain operates, so he has established guidelines for himself that dictate when he is going to study, when he is going to play video games, etc.

This behavior wasn't an overnight occurrence. As the parent, it took me years to get him to the point where he decided that he would do the work necessary to achieve his goals. He used to get angry when he got a lower grade, but when we talked about whether or not he was putting in the effort to achieve the goal, he would admit that he hadn't. It took years, but I had to consistently remind him that he needed extra time to achieve his goal, which meant that one of his other likes-video games, *YouTube* videos, or card games-would have to play second fiddle to the goal that felt more important to him.

We went back and forth on this goal for a long time because we needed to be sure that he was physically capable of achieving it. So I had to monitor his abilities. Higher-level math courses and processing issues don't necessarily befriend each other, so I watched to see the difference between how he performed when he did not put much effort into a course versus when he did. I noticed that when he was just putting cursory effort into the course, he was making high B's, and this let me know that if he challenged himself just a bit, he could get the higher score. I didn't want him to grow up using autism as a crutch, so we talked about the difference between effort and too much pressure, and once he did some self-analysis, he settled on pushing himself to get the grade because it really was within reach.

Now, last school year, he was taking an online AP Physics course. He was really struggling to complete the assignments, but I did not intervene so that he would have the chance to deal with it himself. What happened, though, was that the answers to the questions on the quizzes and the exams had been uploaded incorrectly, and my son was spinning his wheels trying to solve an unsolvable issue.

In that case, I had to intervene because the frustration caused my son to become overwhelmed. Even though I intervened with the teacher, I realized that my son would probably face such issues when he went to college. He would be an adult by that time and would need to be able to cope with those sorts of problems without my assistance, and he would need to be able to solve the problem himself. I also realized that he would face those sorts of issues once he started working. So we went back to his specialists for guidance. I realized that the plan we established for him when he was eleven was not going to be sufficient for him at twenty. So, once again, seeing our specialists for the second time helped us develop a current game plan that we are now using to help him achieve his goals.

Having rules, routines, goals, and expectations provide structure within which children can learn to negotiate life. If I did not have expectations for my son, he would not have goals. If I did not have rules and routines in the household, my son would not know how to manage his time and energy in support of his goal and would probably feel unsuccessful and would definitely be unprepared for adulthood. To sum it up, if we want our kids to be successful once they are adults, we have to obtain a clear understanding of how they function and use that understanding to establish and negotiate doable goals, and we have to establish routines, expectations, and rules that support those goals.

Dealing with Schools

I want to end this book with a few brief suggestions about how to deal with schools when you have a child with autism. I have the vantage point of being a teacher and being a parent of a child needing IEP services. I know how daunting the prospect of meeting with teachers and administrators and specialists can be. But I would like for you to keep your goal in mind. You want your child to do well in school. You want your child to get as many supports as are possible to help him or her access the curriculum. I know that children on the spectrum need lots of support, so don't quit because this is a difficult process. It will be uncomfortable at times, but be tenacious. You can do it.

1. Show up to all meetings scheduled for your child. Be on time to all meetings scheduled for your child. Call to notify as early as possible if you have to cancel a meeting. Keep phone numbers readily available if you are running late to a

meeting. It probably seems unnecessary to say this, but as a teacher, I get calls all of the time telling me that I don't have to come down to a meeting because the parent did not show up. For my own son's meetings, I have been available to have a phone conference when I physically could not be present. I do whatever I can to make sure that I am present when I need to be. So show up. Decisions will be made in your absence, and chances are, you will not like those decisions.

2. This is a business transaction. You may be nervous, upset, and/or concerned, but as best as is possible, leave the emotions at home, and bring the facts. You have to have as much documentation as you can provide to support the requests that you have. Develop clear questions, and plan and practice what you want to say when you speak in the meeting. You will be asked to express your opinion, so prepare ahead of time so that you don't forget important points once you're in the meeting. Be calm, assertive, and respectful. There is no time for sarcasm, there is

no time for being flippant, there is no time for being argumentative- the only focus is getting your child the accommodations he or she needs to be able to function at his or her maximum potential in school. Take specific notes, and read the IEP carefully before you sign it. Make sure that you read the accommodations section so that you know and agree with the supports your child should be receiving.

3. Research and understand your and your child's rights under IDEA. As I stated before, children with medical disabilities have a federally protected right to receive accommodations that will make the educational curriculum available to them. Never forget that. The federal government has a website at www.idea.ed.gov. Review it carefully so that you will be aware of your and your child's rights under the law.

4. You need medical documentation. Your doctor needs to write clear instructions as to what your child needs. I wouldn't see a doctor who is not willing to prescribe for the school the sorts of

assistance that he or she feels are necessary for your child to flourish in the educational environment. Be clear about what you need before you schedule an appointment. Be clear with the receptionist about what you need, and the receptionist can communicate with the doctor to see if he or she creates such reports before you schedule an appointment.

5. Don't let any member of the IEP team tell you that your child should not have the accommodations that you and your doctor have agreed are necessary. Unfortunately, I have had this experience. Teachers and administrators do have valuable experience, but they are not medical doctors. Make sure you have documentation and understand your doctor's suggestions well enough to relay their importance to the IEP team.

6. Check to see if your child's teacher is highly qualified to teach the subject matter. Let's say your child has a written expression disorder, and your child has been placed in a class where a

long-term substitute is functioning as the teacher. You need to find out this substitute's qualifications. For example, if the substitute is teaching English, find out if this substitute has a degree in English or English education. If the teacher doesn't have a degree in a related field, and you see that your child is struggling, then you need to have your child moved. In the same vain, if your child's teacher is qualified but has no classroom management, and your child cannot learn in that environment, have your child moved. Document everything, and have your child moved out of that classroom and into one in which your child can learn.

7. Most educators want to help, but if you face staff members who don't seem to be prioritizing your child's progress, document and seek to speak discreetly with supervisors and administrators both at the school and district/county level if necessary. Currently, my son has an excellent special education team, and I had two excellent special education teachers who worked to get my

son placed in school when we were in Northern Virginia. But there were educators who were not as dedicated to my son's progress. At the end of the day, our job is our children, so make sure you fight to get everything your child needs to be prepared and to perform well because once your child leaves the structure of the school environment, he or she will need to be prepared to negotiate the real world as a legal adult.

8. Do not be afraid to talk to the central office, the school board, directors, etc. about your child's issue if your concerns are not being addressed at the school level. Have your documentation, take notes during meetings, and be prepared to thoroughly discuss how your child is being negatively impacted by any inaction at the school level. You are dealing with your child's educational development.

9. Be involved in your child's coursework. Even when he or she gets to high school, find out what your child is doing in math. Find out about writing assignments. Find out what's new in

science class. You may be able to help the teacher teach your child even better by helping the teacher understand how your child has been thinking or mis-thinking about a particular concept. As parents of children on the spectrum, we behave as interpreters for our children. By understanding our children, we can teach them to recognize the areas in which they need more help and clarification, and they can, in turn, use that information to advocate for themselves as they grow older.

10. Finally, make sure that you and your child are doing your part. Complete homework. Complete assignments. Complete paperwork. Show the teachers and the school that you all are doing your best to ensure that your child receives a quality education.

~

Our life on the autism spectrum

...has been a journey that I never would have believed that I would have to take. Any parent who lives with a child on the spectrum knows how demanding this job is. A lot of people ask me how it is that my son functions better than he used to. My only response is that I was able to get to know him so well that I knew what he specifically would need to get to a level of performance that fit him. Every step that I discuss in the book came about as result of looking at my son's needs and figuring out what would be best for him. I became an expert at him. And that has taken a lot of yielding, a lot of prioritizing, a lot of focusing on him. I have also learned to be okay if tomorrow, he doesn't function so well, if tomorrow, he decides that pushing himself the way he does just doesn't fit anymore. That's okay, we'll just have to go back to the drawing board to figure out our next step.

Our life on the autism spectrum

...has shown me that kids on the autism spectrum need their parents tremendously. They need us to help them navigate this world in a way that requires a lot of selflessness and so much flexibility. And yes, we can do this, we really can.

Our life on the autism spectrum

...has taught me that I am not an island. I am so used to doing things on my own, yet I have not been able to live that way with a child who has autism.

Our life on the autism spectrum

...has taught me patience.

Our life on the autism spectrum

...has taught me to have more compassion.

Our life on the autism spectrum

...has taught me that love is so important, and that we all have purpose, beautiful purpose, for being here.

Our life on the autism spectrum

...has taught me that living in our own skin is just fine, and seeking help when we need it is a necessary part of this existence.

Our life on the autism spectrum

...has forced me to know that I am resilient and can keep on trying to be the best person, the best parent, the best mom I can be despite mistakes and despite failure. I can keep getting up to be better.

For parents everywhere who love their kids